M000204788

MANAGING THE MILLENNIAL MARKET

A Guide to Teaching, Leading, and Being Led by America's Largest Generation

SETH BARNETT

The Seasoned Group, LLC.
New York

Dedicaiton

This book is dedicated to all those that have taken or will take time to hear me speak about Millennials. I believe that the best way to create common understanding among generations is to give someone the knowledge to have an intelligent conversation with someone else. It is also dedicated to my fellow Millennials who I continue to learn much about. As a Millennial, I am so proud of our generation and all that we will do for the world.

To David and TCU Extended Ed —
— thank you for all you
do in education and in
our community.

Seth Barnett

Contents

Acknowledgements ix

1. Introduction 1
2. A Changing World 9
3. The Many Names of Gen Y 17
4. Perception 27
5. Millennials At Work 39
6. Millennial Consumerism 47
7. Social & Public Image 53
8. Millennial Leadership & Value 61
9. Keys To Success 69

Book Seth! 75

Acknowledgements

I want to acknowledge those who helped me see the need for this conversation and continue to support my cause.

- My wife, Jenni
- The entire promotional products industry
- Tim Brown
- Madison Conradis
- Jessica Hutwelker
- Mark Jenkins
- Bruce Perryman

1.

Introduction

B efore reading any further, do me a favor. Think about your present perception of the word "Millennial". Take a moment to really focus on the nuances of that word and what it brings to mind. It may be good thoughts, negative thoughts, you may laugh some; these are all okay.

Even without knowing exactly who the Millennial is, you probably have an image in your mind and some words that you naturally associate with this demographic group. Now expand that thought process to include anyone from a younger generation than you. What characteristics stand out?

Next, think of that image and those words and put them all up on a virtual whiteboard in your head. Get every word on there and get a rough rendering of an image of a Millennial pasted on there, too. Review what you have designed. Now, assign someone who you are in regular contact with to those characteristics, good or bad. It should be a little difficult to do.

The reason I start here is to show that we all have perceptions about one another. Generational demographics are one of many categories of ways we perceive others. I always say that we are each so unique that even the judgements we pass are totally specific to us. You will find in this book that although each generation has their own positives and their own flaws, unfair perceptions can negatively impact the way we interact with one another.

For the sake of redefining your understanding of Millennials, young professionals, the next generation, and the future leaders of our world, do me one big favor. Erase the whiteboard you just created. Remove all your perceptions of Millennials, good and bad. Remove that image of your portrayal of this demographic. I ask you to do this as a way of starting fresh. You may have great examples of teaching, working with, or mentoring Millennials and I am thankful for that. However, most of the generations who are not Millennials, and even some Millennials themselves, have a negative view of this group based on numerous factors. This may be thanks to the media, conversations among your peer groups, or personal interactions you have had. In order to really understand how the Millennial generation is unique and perhaps misrepresented, you must clear away all preconceived ideas, even if only temporarily.

Now, let the following phrase resonate with you and keep it in mind as you read this book and as you work with other generations: "respect goes both ways". Early on I realized that Millennials are often misunderstood in how they interact and engage with other generations. However, I also found that all generations have a similar challenge. We all can be unfairly represented. So, I like to teach people that respect is reciprocal. If you are one who is quick to unfairly label someone of a younger demographic, remember that they can be just as quick to unfairly label you. It is just like the adage that most of us were taught as children: "treat others the way you want to be treated".

Let me take a moment to explain the "why" of this book. I am by no means a generational expert in the scientific understanding of the term. But, I AM a Millennial. Actually, I am a PROUD Millennial. I see the world through a Millennial lens and have lived a very Millennial life up to this point. I consider myself a business professional. I went to college and graduate school and got a job working in the legislative industry, which is what I had sought out. I did that job well for several years. However, I got to a point where I became frustrated by the way people perceived me and the way those from an older demographic chose to interact with me based on their understandings of my generation.

This came to a head in 2015 when I was attending a legislative conference in Seattle. One of the speakers said "the biggest problem businesses will face in the coming years is the aging population". Now, what this person was saying is that we are nearing a mass exodus within the workforce of the United States. The Baby Boomer generation has been the leaders of business, the teachers in our schools, and the foundation of our working class for nearly three decades. But, this massive group is at or nearing the point of retirement. Within the next decade the working Baby Boomer population will be cut in half. So, the biggest problem is that businesses are not well prepared to conquer this challenge.

What I interpreted the speaker to mean when he said the aging population is our biggest problem is that the root of the challenge lies in the fact that we don't have people ready to take on the responsibilities left by the exiting Baby Boomers; but we do.

I came back from the conference with a new approach to helping solve this "biggest problem". My idea was to help people prepare for the Baby Boomer exit by better understanding the generation that is the natural fit to take on these open responsibilities: the Millennials. I knew that the way people perceived Millennials at many different levels was not totally accurate. It was not until I began having the conversation about Millennials in the workforce that I realized that this perception was harmful to the future of our economy.

Think about one person not willing to promote a Millennial to a leadership role within their company because that person has a misunderstood knowledge about the Millennial generation as a whole. Now multiply that by the nearly 20 million business within the U.S. alone and you see the problem.

I began to write a proposal that looked at generational demographics as a way to better understand not only Millennials, but also how generations impact and interact with one another. This is not the first time in history where a shift in generational leadership has happened, but, as you will read, it is the most significant.

My second step in this venture was to look at the conversations that were taking place about Millennials as well as examine the research that was being done. Inevitably, if you picked up or downloaded this book, this is not the first time you are hearing about Millennials. This topic is widespread and often the core conversation regarding the future of industry. I continually find this to be true. This topic is here and now and not going away anytime in the near future. What I did find is that the people having the conversations about Millennials were the wrong people to address the topic. Everyone writing books about Millennials or speaking about them in viral videos were not of the Millennial demographic. There is even a viral video that got millions of views on this topic, and one that I agree completely with, but was delivered from someone of an older demographic. This person states in their dialogue that they know Millennials, they understand them. How could this be? They have never been in this demographic group, they did not grow up in the same world as this group, and they will never be able to live as this group does.

This helps support my arguments about generational demographics and Millennials. Again, I am a Millennial who lives this life every day. I gave a lecture to a college workshop and a professor asked why I was the best person to speak about this topic. My response? "Well, look at me. I am this demographic". The interesting thing is that as I began doing the months of research to start talking about this subject, I found many surprising elements. What surprised me most was how much I agreed with my findings. Not only did I learn a lot about the person I am, but I learned why I am continually proud to be part of this peer group.

I must admit, I have become a little more 'Millennial' since starting this journey. I have found a balance between working professional and young entrepreneur. Where I once would not give a presentation if I were not in a suit and tie, now I will not give a presentation if I must be in a suit and tie. This is not specific to all my peers, but being a Millennial means being who I choose to be and being the person I want others to know. I am sure that people's perception of me personally has changed since I've embraced my new-found individuality, but I am grateful for that. I love when people can be themselves and are not tied in to only what is considered correct by other demographics or their own peer group.

Millennials are really not new. In this book, I will break down what makes a Millennial, taking into account their age, demographic history, and the Millennial culture. Millennials are a symbol. They represent a new, large demographic taking its place in our society and beginning to make decisions that impact the rest of us. So, with that understanding, we have all been Millennials. Think about when you accepted your first job. You were the Millennial. You were a young person, full of ambition, and your unique view of the world was going to help shape the job you did and the people you were around. Remember how tough that was?

There are people who will argue that when they took their first job, and subsequent jobs, they put their head down, did their work, and never pushed back. Now, two things are happening here. Either they have mistakenly recalled their youth, or they are not telling the truth. Everyone had that desire and ambition within them at one time or another. That is why the phrase "what do you want to be when you grow up" exists in our society. We live in a world of choice. We also live in a world of compromise, which is why the 8-year-old that wanted to be an astronaut may be managing a bank today. There is nothing wrong with managing a bank, but at some point, that ambition turned to compromise. It may have been because of their high school grades, or the fact that their parents wanted them to get a "regular job", or that they decided they were not passionate about space after all, but instead passionate about finance. What I hope didn't happen was that 8-year-old turned 22, took a job to pay for their graduate degree in aerospace engineering, and then found that money and stability were more important than their ambition. This is, unfortunately, a story told over and over.

We all have ambition in our lives. Millennials are just at a point where they have more than others. It is a deterrent to many in older demographics, who the Millennial may find themselves working for, because they want an employee who can set aside personal ambition for cooperative achievement. Luckily, there is a way to have both.

I encourage people to reflect on the person they were when they took that first job. Remember the ambition and the desire to achieve against all odds. Remember the determination to make a difference and not let anyone stand in the way. The Millennials are these people. The difference at this point in history is that they won't be told "no" easily. When I am speaking to college groups or at universities, I always ask for a show of hands for how many people want to start their own businesses. I have never been in a situation where less than a third of the group raised their hands. This is ambition. It is the wonder of not knowing what odds are stacked against them and wanting to create something totally unique and exclusive. Think about being an entrepreneur in today's market. This must be tough, but ambition has no standards and no precautions. The reality is that of the students who raise their hands, only one out of every thirty or more will start and successfully operate their own business. It is that drive to succeed that I want to see people harnessing and embracing. We have the ability to let that ambition shine, even if that 8-year-old suddenly chooses to be a bank manager. Their passion for achievement is still in them; it just needs to be brought out.

I want this book to encourage and inspire you. If you are an educator, use it as a guide for your present and future students, as well as your present and future peers. If you are a business leader, use it to understand not only the new workforce but the new market. For anyone reading this book, use it to reflect on the ambitious person you once were and probably still are. Let us work to bridge the generational gap within our economy with understanding and candor. Remove any perceptions you have about those in this young demographic, if only until the end of the book.

When you reach the end, you can add words back to your whiteboard. You can put the image of the Millennial back up. But, what I think you will be surprised by, is how the words have changed and the image that you depict is more reflective of the drive, attitude, and integrity of these young people.

The information provided here is based on a Millennial perspective but I will not go easy on the Millennials that are entitled and are seeking to reinvent what generations before us have created. We live in a world of balance. What has been established in our economy works because our economy as a whole works. What we must do is understand the guiding principles of Millennials and relate them to what works best in the world around us. That is the goal of this book. Not to totally reinvent everything you thought you knew, but to give it a fresh spin. It is my hope that any hesitations you had about teaching, working with, mentoring or engaging those of the younger demographic will be eliminated. I hope to present it to you in a clear and concise way, always keeping in mind that respect goes both ways.

2.

A Changing World

T he world we live in today is constantly changing and evolving. Many factors contribute to how education, business, and industry are adapting to a new, technology-driven, global marketplace. Each generation contributes uniquely to these changes, but Millennials are the drivers of this change. Millennials did not invent technology, social media, globalization, artificial intelligence, or urbanization, but they are the number one contributors to how these things are connected to our everyday way of life.

For decades, businesses have discussed something called "change drivers". These are the elements of society that impact how businesses, large and small, operate effectively. Change drivers are also a significant consideration in education, as schools and universities need to be able to speak to the global adaptation to these change drivers. Change drivers of the past were things like cars, suburbanization, the progression of the phone to the fax machine to email, the internet, etc. When each of these change drivers entered the marketplace, they caused interruptions to businesses and society. Think about it this way: to remain relevant, the carriage driver, who was an expert with horses, had to become an expert with engines when the car was invented.

They had to stay applicable to the changing world and consider the fact that the car was not a passing trend but a new way of life. Another example is with suburbanization. When the car became more mainstream, it was easy for people to live outside of the areas where they worked. Commerce had to shift to allow for businesses to operate within the city centers, and communities to operate away from city centers; a contradiction to how things had been done previously.

Change drivers help advance our society and ensure that we can compete effectively on a global scale. The main change drivers we face today include globalization, technological advances, and generational demographics. Each of these contribute to a new frontier in our society. They allow for adaptation to the status quo and help challenge us to advance the way we live and work. With that, they are also marketplace interrupters.

Change is a frustrating thing. Most people are unaware of how resistant they are to change. All generations have dealt with change and will inevitably continue to deal with constant change based on the ever-evolving global landscape. Even Millennials who are regarded as the main drivers of change in our market are having to learn how to evolve based on their new and changing environments. They are learning balance at the same time as other generations. Yes, Millennials are often more vocal about their resistance to change. However, they are adapting to renewed complexities that we all face with natural resistance.

Globalization

Globalization is the blending of economies and the inclusion of our interests on a global scale. This directly impacts business, commerce, education, and socialization. We live in an ever-smaller world. Where business competition may have at one time been within a city or state, competition is now spread throughout our economy and into others. Globalization is the free movement of goods and resources between various nations and partnerships. Businesses in our economy have sought out global partnerships to ensure a wider reach and better market share. Education is also now global. Students can participate in web and correspondence based programs from a number of international universities. This allows for a greater global understanding, a more unified international market, and an unlimited ability to share information. However, some argue that globalization is too limiting, placing barriers on free trade and increasing global security risks.

The concept of globalization began for the United States more than 20 years ago as a means of improving our global standing and supplying growth opportunities to developing nations. Today this concept is seeing a massive resurgence. Not only is globalization a reality, many are seeing it as a necessity to our way of life. This is increasingly important to understand when it comes to managing the new Millennial market. This is a group of people who obtained their education during the time since globalization was introduced as an obvious solution to international economic woes. This means that not only do Millennials understand globalization, many do not know a world without it.

Globalization impacts Millennials and in turn, the rest of the market through the demand for global practices and cooperation. A key characteristic for Millennials is the understanding of helping their fellow man. They have been raised in a world inundated by knowledge of international communities and have built a familiarity with the idea of making a personal and professional impact on the global community.

We also can attribute the speed of globalization to how our market is presently reactive and how it will become more so with each new Millennial leader. There is no longer disconnect between nations, international businesses, schools, or communities. Because of their levels of connectivity, Millennials will continue to lead the march toward a more global marketplace. Additionally, they will challenge businesses who are not addressing this need and seek to attain change.

Technology

The first technology boom took place during the late 1980's and early 1990's. This was a time when the advent of major technological innovations changed daily life forever. This was due to many factors, including the development of new technology based industries, massive improvements to education in this field, and most importantly, a prosperous national economy that had the ability to invest in these new innovations. This was a time when household and personal computers became a reality for more than half of American homes; a time when the world wide web opened up the possibility to not only have access to endless information, but to share the information with the masses. This was also a time when micro processing gave way to cellular telephones (although their integration with computers would not happen until much later).

Today, we are in the middle of a second technology boom. This one may not have quite as obvious an impact as the first, but the way it is changing society is even more substantial than its distant relative of the 1990's. Streaming information, digital integration and social media are just some of the agenda items of the new technology boom. Consider this: in 2017 the iPhone turned ten years old, Facebook turned 13 and the first self-parking car was on the road less than two years. This era of technology is new and constantly changing.

The most significant component of this newest technology boom that impacts the way other generations interact and engage with the Millennials is social media. Social media was created to be an online networking tool and social space for when people were not able to connect in person. It was quite literally a social media.

This concept has now moved from social to business, education, communication, and a social norm. It is a necessity among Millennials and an increasing necessity for businesses. However, it is not a necessity by chance and certainly not by pure desire; it is one of functionality. Social media has become so vast that it interconnects nearly 80% of the globe. Businesses have begun to utilize it regularly, educational institutions have learned to embrace it so much so that there are now degrees in social media management. Society sees it as a valuable resource for ordinary life.

Millennials are an obvious proponent of technology trends as they are the first generation to grow up in a world with technology. These digital natives have been inundated by streams of technological change since they were infants and have come of age during a time when digital integration was the norm. Knowing this, it is easy to see why Millennials want to incorporate technology into everything they do.

Over the past five years, businesses and universities have begun to see the positive impact of social media. Most businesses that at one point had either sight blockers or bans on social media use at work have now lifted those with careful consideration. There are still companies that block these sites stating that they are too distracting for employees. However, because the majority of businesses have begun to see the positive effects of social media use and integration, this leaves business who do not share similar feelings out of the loop

It is said that most people who have regular access to a computer, tablet or smartphone during the workday will find something to be distracted by online at least once an hour. These are not distractions specific to social media, just specific to the internet. However, social media allows access to company information, new and existing business connections, and a gamut of pertinent information. It would stand to reason that businesses would understand that distraction is a byproduct of the internet, so why not have people find value in their distraction through social media channels? Educators, too, are finding that students can learn and grow their knowledge-base through social media content as opposed to sites that only seek to take up time.

Nearly all Millennials use some social media outlet on a daily basis. It is the aspect of their technological lives that they are most familiar with. So why not find ways to harness that for a valuable outcome?

Demographics

We reside within the most significant generational demographic shift in modern history. Over the next ten years the Baby Boomer generation, which has made up the clear majority of our working global market for nearly three decades, will enter or near a point of retirement. A generational exodus of this scale has never been seen because no generation has ever been as large as the Baby Boomers, until the Millennials. The exiting of Baby Boomers from the workplace leaves a significant gap in leadership that is only able to be partially filled by the much smaller Generation X. Not only that, because education, business and our society changes so rapidly, this generation gap will have an even more significant impact on our world.

The departure of the Baby Boomer generation leaves an obvious void in our working society. The clearest answer to managing this change is by ensuring that the Millennials take their proper place within the workforce, within management, and as leaders of industry so that this shift does not derail our economic integrity. The issue here is that the Millennials have not been as welcomed into naturally filling these gaps. Part of this is due to the assumption that because the Baby Boomers filled gaps from their predecessors, the Silent Generation, the natural progression would be for Generation X to naturally fill the gaps of the Baby

Boomers. However, Generation X is a significantly smaller group than the Baby Boomers. This means that the world the Baby Boomers have created is too large to be governed by Generation X exclusively. The best bet for success is the Millennials.

Millennial involvement in management and leadership roles in industry within the U.S. has been slow to gain momentum. This has become so obvious that now the generational gap is a common topic and is referred to as one of the most significant, if not THE most significant, challenges we face. One cannot attend a conference, lecture, or series on the future of our nation without hearing about the generational gap. Millennials are certainly in the workforce, but looking ahead to the near future and the massive void that will be created in key roles by exiting Baby Boomers, Millennials are not advancing fast enough to gain the knowledge and experience necessary to lead with the same vigor as the Baby Boomers.

Each of these change drivers represents our present world and how it is being impacted. It is up to everyone to understand why the change is happening to ensure that we all progress together. Each of these factors has numerous examples of how they impact everyone. Businesses large and small and educational institutions at all levels impact the way we, as consumers, observe the market. It is impossible to not be affected by one or more of these change drivers. Knowing that, each of us is not alone in this challenge. We all seek to make sense of the changes that directly impact us. The Millennial generation is no different, but of those in the present market, they are drivers of innovation and change. They represent a new frontier in each of these areas and have found unique ways to embrace change to ensure mutual success. In globalization, technology and demographics change the way we see Millennials. We should each be working to build a better understanding of what it takes to embrace change. Our world is small, our technology is vast, and our neighbors are younger.

A Brief Case Study

Though Millennials are still coming of age and make up a minority in most nations, the Millennials in Vietnam have been the significant majority for several years now. As a result, change has happened quicker there than in other countries in which Millennials have not taken their majority spot just yet. Vietnam, as a nation, is rebranding itself under the authority of the Millennial generation. As a nation, they are working on their image; supporting a stable growth of their economy and creating new opportunities for global leadership. Technology has also played a significant factor to the changing marketplace. Vietnam as a nation, spends more time per capita utilizing technology than any other nation. They are doing all of this through a thoughtful appreciation of their past and with their heads turned toward the future.

3.

The Many Names of Gen Y

T he Millennial generation has been called many things in their short history and have characteristics unique to them and their way of life. Millennials were originally titled "Generation Y", as Y was the progressive figure after X, or after "Generation X". The term Generation X was used for decades before being coined to the group born in the sixties and seventies as a moniker for alienated youth. It was first assigned to that group in the early 1960's as a way of identifying the unique generation that would be born of the earliest Baby Boomers. So, when it came time in the 1970's to identify the generation that would follow Gen X, the moniker Generation Y was a natural fit. However, the first members of this group to emerge as young adults did not like fact that Gen Y was simply a continuation of Gen X. In true Gen Y style, they coined the term "Millennial" to emphasize the fact that the clear majority of their demographic group would be influenced by the changing culture leading up to and after the Millennium. Millennial was as unique to them as they were unique to society. The term Millennial has gained popularity in recent years and is now used to describe this group on a global scale.

There are no true defined timelines for generations. Generations did not start being identified until after the turn of the 20th century and even then, no exact dates were assigned to any group. This is because exact years are not the true indication of the uniqueness among generational groups. Their characteristics are more defined by how they were raised, the influences of the world around them, and what aides them as they come of age. For argument's sake, let's assume that each generation is defined by a twenty-year period. So, Millennials would be those born between 1980 and 2000. Again, based on what you read or who you talk to, this figure could change. For the purposes of this writing, Millennials are those with the characteristics unique to our marketplace, our universities and our businesses, and those that came of age in the late 90's and 2000's. This era was unique, and the changing atmosphere was clearly different than the world that Generation X had come of age in. So, don't let anyone tell you they know exactly what dates Millennials are from, because they don't. Nobody has that answer.

Popular culture, especially media influence, has attempted to better define Millennials. In recent years, many terms have been used, including: "the me generation", "the I generation", "the we generation", and even "the entitled generation". Still, Millennial is a coined term that everyone knows and one that I hope my fellow Millennials take pride in.

There have been recent arguments by some in social media and viral videos that said phrases like "Millennials don't like to be called Millennial". Now, I don't know where these individuals are getting their information, but their sources need to be checked. In fact, if anything, Millennials are trying to take back and redefine this term. I can understand the hesitation to the term Millennial as it has some obvious negative connotations associated with it. Millennials are unfortunately associated with ideas of entitlement, laziness, and narcissism, but this is not the real Millennial. Nine times out of ten, those that believe Millennials should not be called Millennial are from generations other than Millennial.

The term "Millennial" can certainly be misused.. Some in this age group are more sensitive to the term than others because they have probably been put down through use of the moniker in recent years. That is because of the negativity associated with the term. But remember, the term was not created to negatively identify a group; it was created to establish the uniqueness of this demographic.

I attended an event geared at all demographics in 2016 and, like many business and education events these days, the topic of generations, specifically Millennials, came up a lot. A common theme was that of the older generation discussing not just how to interact with Millennials, but what to call them. The irony was that no one thought to connect with the present Millennials to ask these questions directly. If they did, not only would they have learned that the term "Millennial" is totally acceptable if used correctly and without bias, but they would have seen that this group is eager to be approached about generational topics. There appears to be a disconnect and maybe even a fear when it comes to not only interacting with this group, but also identifying them by their self-chosen name. I always tell people if they are weary or hesitant about using the term "Millennial" for whatever reason, they need to find someone of that demographic they are already connected to and simply have a conversation with them. They may be pleasantly surprised by what they learn.

Today, Millennials make up roughly a third of the total U.S. working population. Slightly more than one third is made up of Baby Boomers, with the other third consisting of mostly Generation X with some Silent Generation (those before Baby Boomers) mixed in. Within the coming decade, Millennials will take over that majority spot from the Baby Boomers. Not only will they be the largest generation in our market, but also the largest single generation in American history. Additionally, this influx during the critical time when the Baby Boomers are exiting will also result in the fact that Generation X will never hold a majority spot in our market. Thousands of Millennials enter the workforce each day with thousands more set to enter in the coming years. This means that if our way of life is not impacted by the society the Millennials are creating yet, it will be soon. Society is changing and actively adapting to this new generation. Businesses are making considerations to the obvious increase in Millennial decision makers. Needless to say, the ways of "business as usual" has and will continue to evolve . We are at a unique place in history as we bridge a gap between the three dominant generations that has more obvious complexities than any generation change prior. This is not the first time in history we have seen such an obvious shift in our society based on generations. However, this is the most significant. This can be most easily defined when looking at the world the Baby Boomers came of age in versus the world of the Millennial.

While Baby Boomers have adapted to their present world, that adaptation naturally decreases with age. We now face an unprecedented obstacle just when many Baby Boomers, who are leaders in our society, are most resistant to change. Millennials are calling for change now more than ever.

In the middle of all of this sits Generation X. They are best defined as the adaptive generation. This is a group who created a lot of the headaches between Boomers and Millennials. Their major influences include social media, text messaging and the work to live lifestyle. Millennials have worked to define what not only makes their lives easier, but more effective. Often, this is a source of disruption in business and in the workplace. Generation X is attempting to be the glue between the other two generations, while still maintaining their unique influence.

This is not to say that Baby Boomers have not begun to embrace some change. Today, there are more Baby Boomers utilizing social media, Google searching, and text messaging than ever before. Still, there is something sort of comical to Boomers about their embracing these now very "Millennial" functions.

Defining Qualities

Many things can define Millennials; with the most significant defining quality to being that they are all unique. None of us are the same, Millennial or not. But this demographic group is even more unique in their differences than anyone else. Understanding some basics about this group can help to better define them.

The first and most obvious is that Millennials are plugged in. They are the largest users of technology of all demographic groups. This is thanks to them being the first generation who grew up using technology. From the time the first Millennials attended grade school, computers were available. Most Millennials can remember typing and computer classes beginning early on in grade school. The more recent Millennials were even introduced to smartphones and tablets at very young and impressionable ages. This has done more than help them understand technology's functionality; it has defined their very way of life. Those from older generations will often become frustrated by a Millennial's desire to stay constantly connected through technology. But when you consider that this group has never lived in a world without it, you can better understand their dependence. Moreover, they have become the generation to create adaptability to this technology as part of their way of life. Where social media was once an optional lifestyle function, it is now the way of society. Where text messaging was created as a byproduct of developing phones with computer-like functions, it is now the number one means of digital communication. However, Millennials are not the creators of most of this technology; they are just the product of its place in society.

This is also a group that by nature does not support the status quo. They seek to find new ways of doing old tasks. This is not to say that they don't see value in the traditional way of doing something, but they are okay with questioning if what is being done is necessary and totally functional. Because of this, there are challenges created in the workplace with this group that will continually test and suggest changes to the ways of doing business. As time progresses and Millennials take on more leadership roles, we will see this as less of an interruption and more of an opportunity.

One defining quality that has become unique to Millennials in the workplace is their insistence on a balance between work and life. This can often be misinterpreted as an unwillingness to work hard or as a disregard for the balances of work and life that have been established by older generations. This is a group that expects their personal life to take precedence over their professional life. This idea is an absolute balance that allows for work to not interfere with home life. This tends to be more difficult to comprehend as we live in a world of constant connectivity. Most of us carry our work around with us in our phones. However, the Millennial group has seen their parents or even older siblings grow up in a world where work is the foundation of all life; meaning that work takes a formative place in our lives and how we live. This group is attempting to find a balance in work and life once again. They want to ensure that there is an opportunity to set work aside and focus on life; to make life the foundation and work a support of that foundation. This is even more difficult when understanding that most people who are in managerial and supervisory roles do not share the same sentiment.

With this, Millennials also want to ensure that their personal time is understood by those they work with and by those that seek to do business with them. It is easy to abuse personal time because of connectivity and most Millennials are never truly unplugged.

Therefore, an achievement of work and life balance is something that everyone must embrace.

A Brief Case Study

The understanding of a work/life balance is greatly demonstrated in many European countries. Most nations, such as the United Kingdom, have found that leaving work at work allows them to enjoy lifestyle opportunities more. In fact, because of this, people are often more unplugged in general. There is a common understanding that work time is work time and home time is for family and friends. Most Europeans who abide by this notion even find it entertaining that Americans are such workaholics.

The Millennials are notably the why generation. This came from their very early childhood development when parents encouraged children to ask questions about anything and everything. Many parents can relate to memories of their children asking a question and, with probing curiosity, asking a series of follow-up questions. This was a means of childhood development that was encouraged by parents and teachers early in many Millennial's lives. Because of this, the Millennials are still asking why. Again, it can be a frustrating thing but truly positive if embraced correctly. This is a very curious generation that seeks out answers to every question. Often this is misinterpreted as disrespectful, especially in the workplace. But remember, they are attempting to find areas of personal and professional improvement in every question asked. It is also an inherent need to find solutions.

The Cycle of History

This is not the first time a new generation has emerged while there are large contingents of other working generations in the market. In fact, this pattern has continued to repeat itself throughout history. When the Millennials first entered the marketplace, there were three significant generations present and active. These included Generation X, the Baby Boomers and the Silent Generation. The differences between those of the Silent Generation who came of age during the late forties and early fifties, and the Millennials who came of age during the early 2000's, is staggering. It is inevitable that certain marketplace interruptions would naturally occur when you are dealing with a workforce of people who have worked to maintain order, and a generation whose inherent desire is to disrupt order. But this occurrence was not new when the first Millennials took their place in the market, and it will not be new when the next generation takes form.

There is always a space of about fifty years between the oldest and youngest in a market. This is a phenomenon that has only been studied recently, but its understanding goes back millennia. Generational identification is new as of the twentieth century, but studies of generations can be found throughout ancient philosophy. The study of the impact and importance of generations came about during a time when sociology was being used as a tool to better explain our present status and give society an outlook for the future. With that new knowledge, the variability between working generations emerged and demonstrates that Millennials are not the first of their kind.

There has always been a "Millennial" type generation active in our market. This is a generation that is characteristically unique from those that came before them and, by nature, they cause some market interruption. Take the Baby Boomers as an example. They are the group most immediately affected by the influx of the Millennials. However, they were once a very similar generation. When the Baby Boomers began entering the market in the late 1960's, they were met by a world of conformity and uniformity. But, like most of us have learned about the free loving, peace seeking Baby Boomers or the 60's and 70's, they wanted to create a new and better world. Now think about the contrast between those Baby Boomers and the G.I. Generation of the early 1900's which was well established in the market and had created marketplace empires in a post-depression America. One can only assume that these Baby Boomers caused a few headaches.

It is easy to place Millennials into a specific category of unfair disruption. However, it is also easy to see that they are not the first of their kind. It is even more easy to draw a direct line between the Baby Boomers and the Millennials, as most Millennials were raised by Boomers and have that same desire for change that was instilled in them by their parents. But again, the irony is that Baby Boomers are traditionally the ones who understand Millennials the least. The common issue here is that the world the Baby Boomers entered and began to leave their mark on is a different world than the Millennials are entering today. But the desires are similar, as is the level of resistance.

Today, this market interruption is amplified by things like continuous streams of information, technology access, and mass media; though the effect on the market by the Millennials is relatively similar to other, young generations. We were all "Millennials" at one time or another. It is easy to forget the young, impressionable person that we all started out as. It is also easy to forget that Millennials are uniquely resistant because of how they have been raised by their Baby Boomer parents. Most Boomers don't realize it is the world they worked to establish that Millennials appreciate and want to change for the better. Millennials don't want to recreate the wheel, but they do want to work to improve its use.

4.

Perception

T he number one issue fueling the misunderstanding between generations is perception. Perceptions and projections of each other are unavoidable and ultimately cause confusion, especially among generational groups. This is not just how the older generations perceive the younger group. This is over all generations and between any variety of people. There are obvious nuances about each of our generations that have stuck with each group and may be unfair characteristics for each of us individually. Everyone has had to deal with these in their own way. The Baby Boomers had a tarnished image to the older generations when they came of age, but that image was unfortunately carried by each member of the group, regardless of whether it had any individual merit.

Perceptions are not always harmful. Many of the ways we see each other and create assumptions can be impactful to our understanding of people as individuals. Millennials are the most immediate target of misunderstood perception today. In fact, this causes the majority of tension and confusion within the market. Many don't realize that because they have adopted a certain image of Millennials based on any number of external factors, they have actually hurt their ability to succeed when working with this group. Many of these images have been created through Millennial misrepresentation in the media with a basic misunderstanding of how Millennials work and what they desire out of relationships. Often being able to work with and interpret Millennials is as easy as taking a new approach to perceptions.

The Trophy Kids

Again, some perceptions are not necessarily harmful, but may have an unrealized effect that can be detrimental to the group they refer to. The first and most obvious example I can give about this is in the phrase "everyone wants a trophy". More times than I care to remember this has been said to me in reference to Millennials. Though not entirely harmful and even somewhat comical, this phrase and its meaning can tarnish the reputation of the younger generations. So, for those that don't know the details of this statement, it essentially refers to the assumption that Millennials want trophies for everything they do because they were the first group to get a trophy for everything. Think about it; participation trophies, 3rd and 4th place trophies, attendance awards, improvement awards, and so on. So much of the Millennial generation's youth was defined by trophies and awards that it became inherent.

Two factors are at work with this perception. The first is that the trophy desire is not the fault of the Millennials, and secondly, it is not entirely false and can even be seen as positive. Many argue the fact that they don't understand why Millennials have an inherent desire to be rewarded for mediocrity. It is an unfortunate thing that trophies and awards ever got to the level they did. But remember, it was not the three-year-old soccer player that demanded the participation trophy when they came in dead last, it was their parent's insistence. So, try to not blame Millennials; they could not help it. Research can actually be drawn back to the early 1980's when parents were first told that in order to establish a desire for achievement in their children, they needed constant reassurance and praise. This lead to more trophies and achievement milestones in everything a child did.

Now, let's look at the positive outcomes of this impact. Because Millennials were surrounded by a world that praised their achievements, as trivial as the achievement may have been, it created a desire to be rewarded. Fast forward to the present, and this desire is still within the Millennials. Only now, the trophies no longer exist. What does exist is feedback, and feedback is a gift. Feedback is the Millennial's new trophy. It may seem counterintuitive to a supervisor to give constant feedback and praise, when applicable, to a younger employee, but it is a must. Remember, this group does not know how to operate without "trophies", so give them "trophies" when they earn them, in the form of constructive feedback. This can be advantageous. The Millennials have a need for reinforcement and achievement to such a point that society now has a group eager to succeed and seek out praise. This is extremely positive as the integration between the generations amplifies. It creates a sense of competition among the Millennials.

A Hindrance to Success

Society's description of Millennials has become somewhat skewed, and as harmless as these descriptions may seem, they are a hindrance to the success of the younger generation. Society descriptions come from many places and are referenced in numerous ways, but often they are not created from fact but from opinion. Similar to how other generations have described each other for decades, these descriptors are used as a means of attempting to understand the differences in a generation's behavior and their approach to work, jobs, career, purchases, and so on. In order to better meet the new demands of a younger market, it is necessary to understand societal descriptors versus how Millennials would describe themselves based on similar understandings.

In a recent survey of college freshmen and sophomores conducted for this book, I confronted a group of students studying the principles of leadership and brought to them some of the societal perceptions about their generation. This is a group of students that, by university standards, are required to take extensive leadership courses that focus on how to create cohesion within their future jobs and careers. This comes in the form of understanding a foundational approach to leadership that helps guides students' academic and later, their professional careers. Much of their leadership skill set is developed by looking at principles in business ethics and human behavior. Discussions often take place by viewing different business scenarios and having students understand what leadership principles should be applied to each situation. What surprised me is that the behavioral and even ethical components that persist with the present generational divide were not well addressed. Some, such as insubordination, were heavily addressed in the curriculum and often helped mitigate the effects of generational divides in the workforce. Still, the things I was there to address were not heavily discussed.

I approached this class by giving them some facts in regard to societal perception. This included telling them that in a survey it was found that the following four phrases come up most when describing the Millennial generation currently in college:

"They are impatient."

"They only want fame and fortune."

"They are impossible to work with."

"They have no vision for the future."

After addressing these, I had the students reflect on what those perceptions meant to them, given that they were each going to be the newest member of a workplace with a desire to learn and grow.

The students addressed these challenges through group collaboration. They determined that the perceptions were incorrect based on how they perceived themselves, and also showed how these perceptions could be easily overcome. It was as though they were developing a method of natural elimination that would help future employers better understand who they were away from their peer group. In this, students addressed each of the four descriptive phrases by showing an understanding of why the phrase exists in the minds of the older generation, and then describing how it could be overcome.

Instead of referring to their generation as impatient, they countered with the phrase "you may see me as impatient, but that is because I need to be continually challenged". Further explanation of this redirect was given that in fact yes, this group is impatient. But they are that way because they are eager for new things and more opportunities. The need to be continually challenged can be easily misperceived, but it does not have an obvious interpretation. Someone with a desire to be continually challenged is what the workforce is seeking and has a desire to develop.

Next, they looked at the adage of fame and fortune. For whatever reason, this perception comes up a lot. It could be because this is the generation that revolutionized reality TV, or it could be because they have a need to be visible among their peer group. No matter the reason, students changed the phrase to read "it is not about fame or fortune; it is about being remembered for what one does". Again, going back to being challenged, the obvious next step is showing off success. This is a group that has continual access to a stage on which they can show off in the form of social media and digital content. Being able to brag is a good thing because that only allows them to work harder to achieve something greater so that their brag can be more significant than the last person's.

While many Millennials would agree that they can be difficult to work with, all generations have that issue in some regard. When looking at the impossibility of working with Millennials, the students readdressed this by saying "my success is entrepreneurial but that does not mean I am not hard working". The fact that most young professionals feel that they are behind in the workforce will cause them to work harder. However, this too can be misinterpreted as a difficult individual, but allowing for a level of internal entrepreneurial success gives them the ability to achieve, or fail, on their own. No matter what, being able to work toward success will make them better at whatever they are doing.

Finally, when addressing vision, students stated that their "vision can only be seen in their company or organization's growth". So, knowing that Millennials do have vision for their own success but know well enough that individual success is small and overall success is large, only through a company's total success are they truly visionary.

Looking at these from a new perspective can help people to understand why they can be a hindrance to the success of a new, impressionable, young professional. While none of the descriptors listed here are totally false, they have a different outcome and impact depending on the given audience. Millennials are often more sensitive to any barriers defined by the older generations because they are surrounded by certain perceptions that inherently create inability.

Perception is a Two-Way Street

It is easy to misperceive an individual based on the public perceptions of their given generation. The Baby Boomer dealt with this in the 60's and 70's when society created assumptions about the entire generation. The reality is that the assumptions were about small groups of people and were not in regard to each individual. Similarly, the Millennials are finding the same is true.

While society had placed certain presumptions on the group, the fact is that those may only relate to a small group of people, if any group at all.

Perception, even when not negative, has an unusual impact on a group and on an individual's behavior within that group. Millennials are working to mitigate some of the perceptions. We can look at some of the most common perceptions and work through why they exist at all, and then look at how each perception is altered based on the viewpoint of the person making the observation.

Let's look at three very commonly misunderstood perceptions when related to the Millennial group: personal connectivity skills, hard work and employer loyalty. For a fun fourth option, we will also look at technology and how even a positive perception can hurt the success of a generation.

Tech-Savvy

When someone from an older generation is organically asked how they would describe Millennials, the odds are at some point they are going to identify how technologically plugged in Millennials are, and they are right. Millennials are the first generation to be born into a world with personal technological innovations available to the common man. This means that Millennials have never known a world without technology, and because of this, they have been shaped accordingly. Most people between the ages of 22 and 35 can remember when they first noticed a computer in an elementary school classroom. For me, I was introduced to a computer in first grade when my school built a computer lab and introduced students to the modern PC. A short time later, the school would adopt technology into the regular curriculum and I would never again enter a classroom without a computer. So, yes, it is easy to see how Millennials are technologically connected. However, I will be the first Millennial to admit, I know nothing about computers! I was taught to use a computer, to turn it on and load a program; but I have no idea how it works. I have no idea how any of my technology works for that matter. If I have a computer or technology issue, I know who to contact to fix it.

The difference between the technological knowledge of the Millennials and Gen Xers or Boomers is that Millennials did not have the luxury of seeing the beginning of the technology revolution. Either we were not born yet, or we were far too young. I would say that Gen X and Baby Boomers are the true technology masters since they lived in a world where one day there was no personal technology, and then the next day there was. This caused entire groups to actually sit down and learn the technology, not just its usage. Millennials fell short of this because it was more important at the time to comprehend usage rather than programming, troubleshooting, and so on. The benefit that the generation after Millennials has is that schools are developing curriculum to including computer and technology programming and engineering skills.

While the perception that all Millennials are good with technology is not negative, it can be harmful if the assumption is that a Millennial in someone's employ is able to perform advanced technology driven tasks. People will often ask me for information regarding social media analytics or web programming to which I have no response. I believe that this comes from that natural assumption that Millennials must all be great with technology since they are constantly surrounded by it. The truth is, Millennials probably have more technology issues and frustrations than any other generation.

People Skills

It is often said that Millennials lack people skills. This comprehension comes from the disengagement of the Millennial generation as a whole. Based on the constant distractions and interruptions that Millennials face, this argument is somewhat true. Millennials do not possess the same level of interpersonal connectivity skills as generations before them. However, most Millennials would argue that, in fact, they do have people skills, but its measure must be altered.

People skills at one point meant more than a person's ability to interact in person. It was about utilizing a skillset where knowledge about a person created commonality and in turn helped to develop conversations. The Millennials have the best tools for this skillset in their access to social media and online resources. If you think about it, the more knowledge one has about another person, the more likely they are to create commonality. At one time, finding commonality about someone you were connecting to or doing business with was a difficult task. Today, that information is provided for you in a very public way, thanks to resources like social media.

On a weekly, if not daily basis, I find myself turning to social media for any token of information about someone that I can use to develop a conversation. It may be based on a blog they have written, a family trip they just took, or a review they did for a local restaurant. No matter the content, the knowledge gives me a leg up. Yes, I still need the interpersonal skills to ensure I am able to use that knowledge effectively, but this knowledge makes me better at connectivity each time I utilize it.

Think about social media as the 21st century rolodex. The difference in my rolodex in contrast to my father's that I remember from when I was a kid, is that my rolodex can fit much more information than his. Plus, the odds are, if I have done business with someone or had a good conversation with someone at an event, they and I are connected through social media. That is my rolodex and I want to ensure they are in there.

Hard Work

The idea of hard work seems to have the biggest contrast between Baby Boomers and Millennials. Boomers often think of hard work on a scale that is measured with time. Millennials look at hard work on a scale that is typically measured with anything but time. This may include project effectiveness, reliability, outcome, budget, or any number of other measurable outcomes. The problem here is that Millennials are often misperceived as not hard working because they, as a generation, do not measure success based on the clock.

Millennials were born into a world that was very "live to work" minded, where work was the foundation for everything else in life. Now, Millennials are attempting to reform that and create a "work to live" society where life is the foundation and work is just an aspect of it. Yes, work provides the resources to be able to enjoy life, but that is what Millennials are all about; the enjoyment of life, including, but not exclusive to, work. However, this can be easily seen as lazy.

A Baby Boomer may work 60 hours a week and all weekend to ensure that they are able to get everything they need to do finished. In contrast, a Millennial will try to get everything done within a 40 hour, Monday through Friday, week to ensure that they can enjoy their evenings and their weekend ahead. Statistically, people are more likely to procrastinate if they already know they are going to have to work more than usual. So, Millennials are only removing the procrastination. The problem is, without true deliverables, a Millennial that arrives to work at 8am and leaves at 4pm may be seen as less hard-working because they are not giving the same time commitment as someone who came in at 6am and leaves at 6pm. But within that day, the Millennial is doing all they can to work as hard as they can to ensure they are able to maintain a balance between work and life.

Millennials would argue that hard work is actually their most valuable asset. They want to work hard in their job because it took much sacrifice to get it. They were also raised by the Baby Boomers who instilled a sense of pride in hard work. But their measurable outcomes differ from that of other generations.

Employer Loyalty

The issue today in regard to employer loyalty is that career and job choice is more significant than ever. Additionally, Millennials are the most educated generation in history because they have learned to tailor their education to a variety of career choices. In that, employer loyalty has a natural ability to slip.

For Millennials, the natural intersection of their personal value and an employer's value is where their loyalty lies. If they feel an organization does not align with their values, they have the choice to find something else that does. More than anything, they want to have a voice when it comes to expressing what creates employer loyalty. Yes, company culture is important, but nearly impossible to define as each person has a different idea of what company culture looks like. For Millennials, being able to voice their ideas about culture and value will result in a loyal employee.

The majority of Millennials will change careers at some point within their first 5 years of work. This is less the fault of the employer and more the fault of the university where the Millennial was taught. The number of college majors has doubled in the last decade and Millennials often find themselves stuck defining a career path before every really seeing the career first hand. This results in the high number of Millennials returning to school and changing jobs. The best way to combat this is to create more than a job within an organization. No Millennial wants a job for the sake of a job. They want a career and something that works to define them as much as they define it. With that understanding comes employer loyalty.

Final Thoughts on Perception

Perceptions tend to be the easiest disconnect to understand but the hardest to change. I often tell people that if they think they have previously conceived perceptions about Millennials, they most likely do. The best way to combat this is to clear away any perceptions about Millennials before interacting with each Millennial. This will allow for organic interpretations of the person. Remember, misperceptions can be reciprocal.

5.

Millennials At Work

Millennials are a finicky group at work and are known to challenge employers regularly. The reality is all generations, while in their career infancy, were likely difficult in the workplace. Each generation has brought new ideas to work with an assumption that those ideas would be golden to their new employer. The truth is, even the greatest ideas may get rejected by the newest team member, especially when age is a factor. This is just human nature and part of the workplace that society has established.

Everyone has wants and needs at work and finds a workplace particularly appealing if more of their wants and needs are met. However, the bigger the workforce, the harder it is to please every person continually. The majority of millennials are beginning to learn the necessary balance required at work. So why are they so particular about their working environment? The answer comes in many parts and is unique to each person, but primarily has to do with the path the Millennial took to get to their job or career. Most Millennials will have gained some sort of higher education by the time they enter the career world. This may be college, a trade school or any form of advanced training. In that time, they were given (and still are given) the impression that the world is desperate for their ideas, their leadership and their unique guidance. Teachers, professors, and instructors all want their students to succeed. They help Millennials do this by showing them the world they will be entering and giving them the opportunity to see themselves in it. Unfortunately, the truth is, there are very few employers exclusively eager to hire a recent graduate, especially for a leadership role. The hypothetical world that those in college create is not necessarily the reality of what they will inevitably face.

Because of these assumptions, the graduates that are able to find a job are often disappointed by what they find. In this, they become resistant to changing their perception and find themselves less likely to succeed. The contrast is someone coming in with no unrealistic expectations and, consequently, little ambition. The right balance is somewhere in the middle, consisting of a smart, capable young employee with ambition to work and succeed and having no unrealistic expectations about immediate leadership. Yes, they can still add value to an organization, but their definition of value may differ from that of their employer.

At one time this idea of "earning your place" was what set apart peer competition in the workplace. Because many Millennials have false expectations, they assume that they don't need to compete on the same level to earn something more. Again, this is a byproduct of how they were raised and taught. It is also necessary to note that guided ambition is better than no ambition at all.

More than half of Millennials will change their career at least once in their first ten years of work; not just change their job, but change their actual career. Part of this has to do with choice. Twenty years ago, colleges focused on majors that were broad and could be tailored later at the workplace. Now, students can study very specific concentration areas to help align themselves with their prospective role. Two problems persist with this. First, you don't really know what a job entails unless you are in it on a daily basis. Second, the more specific a concentration, the less options that will be available for work. For example, a marketing major could potentially be everything from a sales person to a graphic designer, while a fashion retail marketing major is going to have more obvious limitations. You will hear again and again how someone of this generation acquired a specific degree but did nothing with it. Let's face it, there are more jobs in sales and graphic design than fashion retail marketing.

This idea that Millennials will leave an organization after a short time is a frustrating reality, and rightfully so. Companies make an investment in people and get them prepared to do their job well. They don't want someone who becomes less content by the day. However, again there is a balance. Look at what a Millennial really wants out of a job, beyond what their diploma may say. They want a culture they can relate to and a team they can communicate with. If both of these elements are in place, they will overlook the fact that their ideas might not be heard or that they are not necessarily in a role to lead others.

Culture at work is an impossible thing to define. Companies try and fail all the time. If a company believes they have the perfect culture, they don't. Culture at work is defined differently by every person. It is easy to create a sense of culture through employee satisfaction, but impossible to give every single person what they want. One person may define a culture as communication, to another it may be the actual working environment.

For Millennials, the definition of culture varies just as much as with any other generation. However, some things stand out that are unique to this group. The first, and probably most important, is communication. This is a group who has been raised in a world of communication and feedback. They crave the opportunity to communicate, both formally and informally, while at work. Open work spaces thrive among this group. If there is an opportunity to freely communicate, productivity among this group will rise. This also speaks to how this demographic relates to supervisors. They want an equal level of open communication with supervisors as with anyone else. This is the "open door, ask me anything at any time" mentality. It creates a sense of inclusiveness and gives them the opportunity to receive regular feedback.

Millennials also desire what they define as a "different" working environment. Some companies take this idea to the extreme and add fun activities to the work day to use as a working distraction. Others have adopted very casual office environments. Regardless, this goal is about providing something unique that staff can feel engaged in. Again, the goal is not to alienate anyone, but to be inclusive.

A certain level of continuous engagement is also critically important. This is involving the team or individual team members in decision making. Not only does this help give people a sense of personal value, it gives them a chance to take pride in the company they represent. Engagement has proven to be a key factor of workplace success among the Millennial generation. The most effective companies are ones frequently finding ways to engage employees while proactively thinking of ways to maintain perpetual interest in corporate culture. While each generation identifies engagement differently, Millennials are the most likely to find value in company engagement.

Work/ Life Balance

We presently live in a culture with a "live to work" mentality. This is where work is the foundation of all other elements in life and, more often than not, work takes priority over many other aspects. This makes sense when understanding that people spend more time working than doing anything else in life. However, Millennials are attempting to take back the work and life balance. They would like to see more of a "work to live" society where work is only a vehicle to create and maintain a desirable life. They want a true balance between the two.

Millennials know there is a 24/7 expectation of them to their friends, their family, and even to their work, because of the level of connectivity adopted by most of the group. For work, they desire the opportunity to leave work behind, both literally and figuratively. Some may choose not to do this. They may go home and continue to check emails on their phone, but the focus should be on their desire for that opportunity. This takes an adjustment in expectations from the company and the supervisor. This group wants to be able to have a life outside of work and to not cross over between the two. Part of that is how they were raised; often in homes with constantly working parents. The other part is the place most Millennials are in their lives and careers. They are working to define their work and life expectations and ensuring they don't set themselves up for failure in either factor. For them, personal life is going to take precedence over their professional life. This doesn't mean that their professional life is not important. It means that while they are willing to work hard on their career, they will work harder on their life outside of work.

Attractive Employer

So, what makes an employer attractive to a Millennial? First and foremost, no one wants a job for the sake of having a job. Millennials want a job that will turn into a career. Yes, their expectations are high for what they want at work, but that is because they want to see themselves working there for an extended period of time. This is not a group that will continue to work somewhere if they are not content. They have options and choices like no one before them had. They want a career and they want a career plan.

At one time career progression looked like a path to climb on a corporate ladder. That is not necessarily the same path that

Millennials are looking at, but no one wants to work in the same job, with the same title and the same pay forever. A career means being able to understand what could lie ahead. This also allows for achievements to be met. Career progression is the foundational element for this demographic at work. This is knowing that with hard work and dedication, something more can come. This conversation has to take place rather quickly with this group. They want to see that something more could be achieved even if that achievement is somewhat unlikely. This is a career roadmap; a chance to show what progression opportunities may be available. Now, most Millennials have a hard time seeing more than five years out, especially in the beginning of their career. This is because there are too many unknown factors. Will that person get married? Will they have kids? Will they need to move for their spouse's job? Anything past five years is too hard to grasp. However, those next three to five years should be defined. This helps them realize that not only is there some stability in their job, but that there is an opportunity to achieve continuous progression. Within career progression is professional development. Today, more companies are providing opportunities for employee professional development than ever before. This helps the employee define a career path by getting involved with others in their career outside of the confines of their company. This also helps Millennials see that perhaps the grass is not always greener on the other side.

Next is compensation. Compensation is still an important factor for this group's career, but unlike the three generations before them, it is not the most important factor. Remember that this is a group that understands hardship. The clear majority remember what the most recent economic recession looked like and how it affected them or their parents. With this, they understand the importance and value of money. They want to achieve and create career success, and compensation is an integral part of that.

While the idea of work and life balance fall somewhere towards the top for most Millennials, another important consideration is the value they see in the company they work for. This may mean that they want a company with a corporate value that closely matches their own, or they at least want that company to have a positive reputation. Most Millennials will do their due diligence prior to interviewing with a company and determine if value relatability is there. However, they also want to continually spot check their company and, as the company values change, ensure that they agree with the changes and advocate for them. This allows for that idea of culture to blend with the working capital of the organization.

The Millennial employee believes that a good company to work for is one that can see the bigger picture; one that doesn't focus exclusively on day to day operations, but shows their employees that they have a vision for the future. Millennials are just as interested in how a business develops employees and contributes to society as they are in any other consideration. That is because each of those elements ensure that not only will the employees be taken care of, but the reputation of the company will be taken care of.

A company that actively develops its people and their careers gives their employees a career full of possibilities. Before a Millennial even comes in to interview with a new company they will know if the company places the utmost value on the people that make the work possible.

Secondly, Millennials want to work for companies that give back to the communities they serve. Another inherent value that many Millennials have is the need to give back to their fellow man. They see this as easily achieved through a company that understands the value of giving back. Most companies contribute in some way to society. However, at least for Millennials, this is measured in more than money.

Success is defined by rewarding relationships, work and life balance, and continual opportunities to learn and grow above all other factors. Giving an employee the chance to find these things will create loyalty and add value.

6.

Millennial Consumerism

F irst things first when looking at the consumer habits of any generation; once again we must remove some perceptions. Many people assume that because Millennials are technologically plugged in that they exist exclusively in a digital world. As you will see, they are driven by digital connectivity, but that does not mean that they only want to do business with their computer screen. In fact, most Millennials crave connectivity as part of being a consumer as a consequence of a world that has become increasingly digital.

The "online" perception about the Millennial generation as a consumer group is misinterpreted. There is certainly an ease that has been established by the companies who rule the digital marketplaces. In the coming years, we will only see more of this, especially as younger generations become more familiar with these online resources. With that in mind, as a society we must work to preserve what we can in the personalized, interconnected marketplace to ensure that not everything has a home in cyberspace.

Millennials are a unique group. They fall somewhere between

modernist and traditionalist consumers. The modernist seeks to have more instant gratification and a total ease of commerce. This means they live in the digital marketplaces and everything from clothes to groceries are better found online. The traditionalist wants to not only seek out their consumer items, but they want to ensure value, price, and quality while maintaining even a minimal relationship with those they are purchasing from. Millennials have adopted many principles from each of these groups, and are not exclusive to one. A Millennial seeks ease of access, but specifies their consumption based on what the product or service is. Something that needs to be purchased quickly, for example, may be bought online regardless of overall value. However, something where there is a need for assured value would be purchased in person after careful review. There is also value in the ability to create and maintain relationships through the consumer process; something the online world is presently missing.

There are not many people that are solely about instant gratification, Millennial or otherwise. Society has made us all more impatient as consumers. Consider this: Millennials purchase through multisensory consumption, or they want to see, feel, smell, or otherwise experience, the product they are purchasing. The online market is not able to provide all of these elements. It is also not yet a place of total instant gratification.

Time is still a factor in this generation's consumer habits, but it is not just about the ability to have something instantly. Many argue that the reason people are so familiar with online purchasing is because it satisfies the need to be instantly gratified. However, there is more opportunity for true instant gratification by going to a local store that minute of that day rather than waiting for an online order. So, instant gratification should be amended to look more like quick gratification.

Cost is also important but it is easy to assume that Millennials only want what is cheap. This is a group that is frugal because of the economic environment they have grown up in. This does not, however, make them cheap. Value is the number one consideration in Millennial consumerism. They want products and services that have the most value, not just the lowest cost. This means that they may pay more for a product if it has higher quality or is going to last longer than its cheaper competitor.

Relationships

There is one thing that sets apart online consumption from all other forms, and that is relationships. Millennials are proponents of relationships especially when it comes to spending money. They want to buy from people, not computers. Even the smallest interaction matters here. That short opportunity to connect gives the spending a face. The biggest consideration to the online market is that it has no face and no personality. Relationships are especially important when the cost of the purchase increases. The more money that is being spent, the more interpersonal connectivity is required. There is no real difference here between the Millennial as a personal consumer or the Millennial as a consumer acting as an extension of a business. They often will treat their budgets at work with the same consideration as their budgets at home. But know this, Millennials do not want to be sold to.

This is a smart group of people who are weary of being sold to. They can quickly spot a sales person and will do all they can to avoid them. Let's set up some perspective. A "sales person" is about the sale. They are seeking the means to an end. The way to challenge this is to not be a "sales person". If you are in sales, think about the things you really do for your clients or customers. You are a delivery method of information for your product. You are a relationship builder who happens to specialize in whatever you are selling. Millennials seek available, valuable relationships as consumers. It is sometimes necessary to remove the "sales person" from the salesman.

Case Study

There should never be an "I" in a sale. This is the "I can do __ for you" idea. Millennials, among others, can spot that sales ploy instantly. Additionally, this approach shows that the end point is the entire goal instead of the relationship being goal one. Now, think about how to rephrase the same pitch to sell the relationship first and the product second. Try changing "I" to "we". "We can do __ together." This shows that you value the connection with the person and the relationship first and foremost. Plus, you are showing that you value what they are involved with just as you want them to value what you have to say.

Online

Online resources can help create and maintain customer loyalty without being totally exclusive to the digital market. Those who do business strictly online are missing out. Equally, those who are doing business with no online presence are also missing out. The key to success is a balance between the two worlds.

Social media and proper digital integration give young consumers a place to connect in a familiar environment. It also allows the company to build up their loyalty base and show what sets them apart from competition. Relationships can be fostered in a digital world but should never be limited to it. The great part of social media is the opportunity to stay in front of consumers on a continuous basis. It would be easy to miss out on the relationship-building tool that is social media by not being involved here. For this demographic as consumers, there is not an option for no presence in the online world. But remember, the face of a company, product or service is more than a digital image.

Some companies have tried, and failed, to create an effective intersection between social media and commerce. These are the companies that are heavily marketing through social media as a way of driving consumer spending. The problem is that the more advertisements appearing on social media, the less involved people will be. Posting a product and giving some information about it is an advertisement, and a sales tactic that Millennials know to avoid. However, posting the same product in use with a description that is not directly related to the item is an opportunity to create relevancy and is not necessarily an advertisement. Many large corporations have this down. They do not market their product or service, but rather the world that surrounds those products or services. This helps create an image of familiarity and relatability without directly selling.

FOMO

Many Millennials will tell you that FOMO, or the fear of missing out, is a real thing. This is the idea that missing out on something has an impact on the person who is left out. Social media and the digital world have created an avenue for success in this. A strategy here is to show those you are connected to that your company, product, or brand does something that someone else may find interesting or even be jealous of. This creates a sense of wonder and drives the person who feels they are missing out to inquire further. Driving traffic back to you, your site or your social media pages is the way to win this game.

7.

Social & Public Image

The best way to maintain standards among Millennial employees, consumers and users is to maintain and protect your social and public image. Conversely, I would tell Millennials the same thing about their public image and how easily it can be tarnished. The world is connected and any move by a company, large or small, is monitored by someone. This is often the source of stress for companies but also is the secret source of success. If Millennials are a digital generation whose consumer access point is online, it is good to have an online presence. However, those that truly stand out are the ones who easily demonstrate how they are living true to their values and mission via digital resources.

It is easy to see how quickly a reputation can become disrupted based on the access to content and information. When looking specifically at a group who utilize social media for so much research and business comprehension, the smallest dispute can stand out in a major way. At the same time, prideful moments can also stand out and help to develop the success of an organization or product.

Adopt an Omnichannel Approach

Linking a company's website, blogs, social media pages, and other online resources together is the basic foundation for developing an omnichannel approach. However, it is only the very start. Some feel that this means ensuring that a web page shows easy access to social media pages, and that those social media pages contain contact information. In fact, it is so much more.

A company's website is the heart of the social and public image world. It is the foundation of the company and an expression of the company's value and credibility. If someone is doing business with you, or is considering doing business with you, at some point they will visit your website. The website is where content such as a company's corporate values, its mission and its vision are located. Social media is the place to make that value, mission and vision a reality. It is the place to show how the company physically embodies what they claim to be.

The best business social media pages, to a Millennial, are ones where the value of the company comes to life. If a company states that part of its value is giving back to the communities that the company works within, the social media page should show the embodiment of this in the form of imagery and content about community service acts being done. Even if the company is not in the business of helping the community, if the say it, they had better show it. Additionally, if a company shows that it believes in the quality of its products, social media should show what that looks like. It could be an inspection at a factory or a note from the Consumer Product Safety Commission about credibility. No matter what, social media should show the lifeblood of the company.

Millennials are extremely attuned to which companies have a proper omnichannel approach to their public content. They increase or decrease loyalty to a company or a brand based on how well the brand lives its core value. Just as easy to see how a company expresses its value, it is easy to see the ones who don't. These are the social media pages that look as though they have not been touched. Remember, it is better to not have one than have one that you do not use. If the first place a Millennial goes to research a new company or to learn about a brand is social media, there needs to not only be something there when they complete the search, but something there with value.

Stay Social

Remember that Millennials are interested in how a company develops itself and social media is the best tool to demonstrate that. When social media was created, it was truly an access point of social interaction. In recent years, it has become a necessity of the modern business world. Still, these resources maintain their effectiveness by being social. Companies misinterpret effective social media use as an extension of their website. This means that the social sites will have similar content as the website with nothing social about their postings. The content that is critical for social media is that which inspires the user to be social. It is difficult to be social on a page that only lists products and services and doesn't demonstrate that they are living their core values.

The best content creators as companies are ones who inspire action. Action can be as simple as a social media "like" or something that inspires people to repurpose the content to ensure others see the value. The good thing is that if a company website is a suit and tie, social media is shorts and a t-shirt. It is a place to be more relaxed about content that is being created. Yes, there are certain standards to maintain, but it is more of an open canvas for creativity and connectivity. The better and more frequent the content that is generated, the more attraction a company will have.

Wouldn't we all like to invite our clients, customers and colleagues to a big beach BBQ? Social media should be the digital version of that. A place to give back, connect and be happy.

Social Media Standards

Most of us remember a time not too long ago when social media was seen as strictly "social". This meant that there was no place for it at work and many companies had policies that banned social media while on the job. Today, thanks to advances in technology and the necessity of social media as a business medium, companies not only have begun to lift these bans, but have elminated policies that promote proper social media usage. Millennials are certainly heading up this cause.

Because most Millennials have seen the evolution of social media from another social channel to a regular part of life, they understand the effectiveness of it as a research tool and a business aid. More importantly, they see it as such a norm that it becomes very obvious when a business or individual is not on social media. For me, social media has become the more integrated part of my life where my business and pleasure world meet and effectively communicate. On the business side, I utilize social media more as a place to store information about people I have met and interacted with, much like a business card notebook once did. The truth is, I get thousands of business cards every year and the odds of me keeping tabs on all of those people and their companies strictly through their business cards is slim. But, thanks to the power of social media, if I can utilize online tools to connect and even communicate regularly with these people, it allows me to take those critical relationships to the next level. The truth is, a person who truly believes that relationships are a foundation of their business would be most effective by utilizing some form of regular communication with all the people they interact with. Social media does that for us, and even if it doesn't give a stream of insight, you are always one name or company search away from picking up that relationship where you left off.

Today, the average social media user will check one, if not all, of their social media pages at least once a day. Each time they do, that is a potential opportunity for you or your business to leave an impression. There is no other communication method that can give you those odds.

Because of the constant connectivity of social media through mobile devices and the regular access most people have to computers, social media is now a critical tool for effective business. There is not a single Fortune 500 company that doesn't have a social media manager in some capacity. These companies understand that this level of connectivity to stakeholders is unmatched. Plus, now you have Millennials that use social media not only to research and review companies and as part of constant connections, but as an alternative communication method. This can come in the form of a direct message or a post where the company or individual is mentioned. This shows how important it is to continuously monitor social media pages and ensure that the necessary level of communication is upheld. Many Millennial consumers do not see the differentiators between text message, email and social media chats. This means that they may have a preferred method of communication through one of the social media channels and expect the same level of engagement and timeliness as they would get from a phone call or email.

Winning at Social Media

Businesses often struggle with social media integration into their marketing and communications plans because it can a daunting task to start up and complete properly. Additionally, many businesses don't have the resources to hire someone to take on the social media responsibilities or find someone who can consult with their team. However, some valuable solutions for creating, integrating and even updating existing social media plans include:

- Social Media Take Over: A social media take over can be done within an organization through a committee or board. This is where different people are given access to the company's social media accounts and tasked with creating content, increasing visibility and developing new tools. The time frame can vary, but the objective is to take a social media page that is new or lacking in visibility and increase its productivity by improving the quality of content that is being produced. This can be through resource sharing, pictures and videos of the company or clients, or through any number of fun and creative ways to improve overall value. The great thing about tasking this to different people at different times is that the content will vary based on the individual manager. It also allows the responsibility of social media to be passed along. This can be done by continually rotating the content manager in the organization, or having an end date. Perhaps someone within the organization has shown that they would enjoy taking on the responsibility more permanently. Remember, to many, social media is enjoyable and not seen as a burden.

- Social Media Intern: Interns are a great way to tackle social media. A marketing intern could be given the opportunity to not only manage this program, but to be a unique content creator. An intern could come in and spend their time establishing not only a valuable social media page, but could also work to define a social marketing plan which could then be adopted by the organization.

I often get asked about the connection, or disconnect, between personal and professional social media pages. The truth is, social media visibility is the most important, no matter if this comes exclusively from the company or from the company and its employees. Many people want to separate out their personal and professional lives on social media. This is an absolutely acceptable approach. However, as a Millennial, I choose not to distinguish between the two. The truth is, I am not going to post anything to social media that wouldn't be something I would bring up in conversation with someone. So, I may have personal and professional elements throughout my social media pages, but that is a reflection of who I am. You will find that many Millennials take this approach. No matter the case, presence is critical.

8.

Millennial Leadership & Value

It is foreseeable that our future will succeed or fail in the hands of America's largest generation. The following content speaks to those future leaders and their present undertakings. This is not necessarily a section to skip over by those in a generation other than Millennial, but one to learn from. Millennials are at an unique and defining point in their history. Many Millennials that read this are already in leadership roles and looking to take on more responsibility. Others may be recent college graduates still trying to figure out how they can achieve their career goals and yet maintain their individuality.

For My Fellow Millennials

I hope that you are as proud to be a Millennial as I am. We are unique and our generation is the most diverse, educated, and ambitious of any before it. It is my hope that if you desire to change the world, that you can succeed in doing so. This may be the world immediately around you, but you have the ability to leave your mark on society and proclaim that you are an important part of our intricate culture. But this comes with balance and understanding. We are misunderstood by most of society who are not Millennials. In fact, we are the most misunderstood group to ever hold a significant spot in the market. This is a frustrating challenge to those of older generations who are doing their best to learn our nuances and adapt accordingly. But for us, it is just as much of a challenge entering and leading in a world that places certain interpretations on our group.

First and foremost, it is my hope that you are able to hold your head high as a Millennial though you may be surrounded by those that make you feel alienated within your own generation. We should not be ashamed of the challenge we are placing on society with our influx. We do this as a means of advancing our world and ensuring that our future is secure. We have also been raised in such a way that personal and intellectual education is turning into results. Still, we are entering a market that has become well-established without us. This means that we must be careful about making suggested edits.

The age of the Millennial is upon us, meaning that in the coming years the shift to a majority Millennial market will be unprecedented. In 2017, our generation made up roughly one third of the U.S. marketplace. Within the next decades, we will pass Generation X and the Baby Boomers to become America's largest generation and bring with us all the ambition that comes with Millennial leadership. At no point has a generational shift been so present, so significant in size, and so widely misunderstood. With this shift comes enormous responsibilities to our society, our economy and our world. We are now in a place in history where the last of the Millennials are nearing college graduation. This means that once these last Millennials take their place in our market, the challenges to other generations and defined society will be the most impactful. So, it is up to us as a generation to ensure that everything we are doing comes from a place of societal understanding and balance.

Millennials as a generation are a brand unique to our market in such a drastic way that their brand's impact is the most substantial of our time. A brand is something that defines itself uniquely from other similar products. In this case, other generations represent other competitive brands. For a brand to stand out in a way that gains positive attention from consumers, the brand must understand the competition. Yes, all generations are cohesive and work most effectively toward success as a unit. But make no mistake, there is competition among our generational brands, and Millennials are currently losing. Think about what makes one brand stand out from another and why you value one more than another even when the product is similar. People are choosing to hire and do business with older generations more than Millennials because of the brand reputation of the older generations. These generations have had time to create dominance in the market, and because of the uniqueness of the Millennial brand, it is a risky investment. However, that perception is changing through Millennial growth and leadership. Still, in order to understand how to market a brand properly, you must understand your competition.

Baby Boomers

The most obvious competition that Millennials face today is the Baby Boomer generation. This generation is most removed from us in every aspect and will show the most brand resistance. It is most concerned about our leadership methods, though the irony is that 90% of us were raised by Baby Boomers. It is in their pride for being the most dominant generation in the world for more than three decades that this group established such a reputable brand. The Baby Boomers were the result of a post-war population spike that began in the late 1940's. The world had never seen an increase in population on this scale before. Plus, because much of the world was involved in the Second World War, this was felt in nearly every corner of the globe. Coming of age, this group was an obvious departure from their parents who were conservative in nature, prideful in their societies, and stood for economic growth and prosperity at all cost. As the Baby Boomers entered the workforce and began defining their brand, they were very opposite of their parents' generation. They rejected authority and believed in unity over progress. But as time progressed, their brand image changed. With age came more conservatism, and as time progressed they became more socially confident. This created an obvious internal struggle with Baby Boomers, and one that would then be given to their children.

What is interesting is to see how much of the Baby Boomer's youth mentality was passed on to their children and ironically causes them so many headaches today. They instilled a sense of community in their Millennial children in such a tremendous way that now Millennials have an inherent need to be constantly connected. Though many Baby Boomers have strong opinions about social media and personal technology, it was their inspiration that created a need for the present level of continued connectivity.

It is inevitable that Millennials have had and will have significant interaction with those in the Baby Boomer generation. Most Millennials will work for or be supervised by Baby Boomers within the first ten years of their first job or career. Because of the present generational shift, younger Baby Boomers will inevitably work with or even work for a Millennial at some point over the next decade, if they don't already. It is easy to understand the natural tension that is present between these two groups. However, each must work to seek out commonality to ensure mutual success in the coming years.

Generation X

The next competitors are ones that bridge the gap between us as Millennials and the Baby Boomers as world leaders. Generation X is considered the middle generation as they are the middle between the two largest generations. Those that are middle children can attest to the fact that it is a definite challenge being between an older person that has forged their own way and created exclusive success, and a younger person that has been given the most immediate attention by the parents. This is no different than what Generation X is experiencing right now. They seek similar success as Baby Boomers while attempting to stay one step ahead of the Millennials. This is amplified by the fact that Generation X has never and will never hold a majority spot among generations. This is also the most competitive generation among us. As any middle child can attest, the need to be overly competitive is part of survival. Generation X is attempting to stand out to Baby Boomers, while developing their own ways of doing things, and ensuring that they define themselves as leaders to those younger than them. Because of this, natural competitiveness is unavoidable. Generation X is also the most adaptable generation in that they understand that cooperation means success. Yes, they would like the world to be unique to them, but they understand that there are multiple generations at work and that their success means success for everyone.

Generation Z

The newest generation to emerge is Generation Z, the generation that follows the Millennials. Little is presently known about Generation Z and how they will react to or challenge our already changing market because few from this group have taken a significant role within the market. Still, Generation Z will be the biggest competition for Millennials as they begin their careers. The amount of shared knowledge, education, marketplace understanding, and resilience will only increase with time. In that, Millennials are already feeling the weight of Generation Z. Only time will tell what impact this generation will have on the market. Though they will never be as large of a group as the Millennials, they will continue to challenge the world around them with similar vigor.

Millennials

Your fellow Millennials may be the biggest competition that you will face in the present and distant future. This is a group that is not only competing against you in society, but seeking out the same opportunities as you. It is likely that at some point in the beginning of your career you will have to answer for being a Millennial based on a perception that was created by your generational peers' behavior. Additionally, some research suggests that there are actually two Millennial groups; one that represents those born before 1990, and one that represents those born after that date. Characteristically, all Millennials are similar based on when they came of age and the world that is beginning to accept us all today. In reality, there are many groups of Millennials that are unique to their background, their socioeconomic status, their culture, and so on. But this can be said about every generation at any point in history. Your real competition is each one of these fellow Millennials because they are working just as hard to stand out to future employers, supervisors, and business connections.

Think about your competition when you applied for your first job out of college. The words on your resume looked very similar to those of your classmates and your immediate peer competition. There is nothing that makes you stand out among everyone at that time, even if you have all the collegiate accolades one can have. What does stand out is your individuality and character. However, true individuality is difficult to express on a resume. This is where Millennials have competitive advantage among the workforce. The chances of someone being called in for an interview based exclusively on the words on a resume is slim. Many employers do more extensive searches to learn about potential candidates. Some ask candidates to fill out personality assessments while others will ask for social media links and anything else in between. What they are attempting to do is understand who the candidates are away from the words on the resume. Knowing that, the candidates that stand out the most are those with the most to show for their character and their value. The words on a resume do not hold as much credibility as one's demonstration of their own character and their value.

So how do you, the Millennial, want others to see you? Knowing that there is already perceptions about the Millennial brand, good or bad, will help to understand how to create unity in what we do. No, it is not all about us and what we want to accomplish and the world we want to live in. It is about understanding that our generational competition wants to achieve and succeed just as much as us. With that, we can find balance in our approach by gently pushing for change. Our brand will continue to define us. There are those Millennials who may tarnish the image of our group, but we cannot let the mistakes or misguidance of a few impact us as a whole. Taking pride in our Millennial brand is the start to achieving a more acceptable understanding. We must work to establish a properly prescribed image and impression in the minds of others about our generation.

Your work, career and success are not based solely on the question of what "you want to be when you grow up" anymore. It is not only about what you want to do, but the person you want to be while doing it. What defines success to you helps set you apart from other Millennials and other generations. We each define success differently and have a different idea of how to achieve it. Perhaps success to you is not financially based. Your ultimate story of success will most likely look different than what we were taught success was. Our parents and teachers instilled in us the idea that success meant maintaining a steady job, being an upstanding member of the community, and finding a way to get to retirement with financial stability. Today, success can still have those elements, but it most likely means so much more. Being able to define what success looks like to you gives you individuality and personal value.

The values that Millennials hold close are unmatched. This is often something that has defined each one of us so much that we are not willing to easily let it go. Value can be anything from the type of work we choose to do, to the stores we choose to spend money at, or the brands we stay loyal to. The pride we have in what we see as having value helps to define our brand and its uniqueness. The biggest challenge for Millennials in defining their brand is working in and truly living in a world that does not fully accept them. This is where it becomes easy to sacrifice who we are for a better job, a cheaper price, or for someone else's value. There is a way to hold our values close, be prideful as Millennials, and succeed, but it takes all of us working towards a common goal.

9.

Keys To Success

There are many necessary elements required to act on this new knowledge. The biggest and most effective is to begin a conversation based on these principles. This could be making a connection with a Millennial to inquire about their viewpoints, or it may be seeking someone out who has been frustrated by the marketplace changes being delivered by this demographic, or it may be broaching the subject with staff. No matter which one it is, the way to bridge the generational gap is to talk and to listen.

Streamline Online

It should now be clear to you that we are all products of our environment. Millennials, being products of the most technologically advanced three decades in history, are by nature, technology driven. Due to this, much of Millennials' success in businesses comes from an understanding of the value in modern technological communication. We must all embrace the fact that this newest technology boom has impacted our business and daily routine more than anything before it. Twenty years ago, people were trying to determine if websites and online marketing were really as important as some were making it out to be. Today, we find ourselves asking the same questions about digital communication and social media. Like any revolutionary communication tool, whether the newspaper, the teletype, or the fax machine, there is value in the advanced way of doing something. I cannot say with any certainty that social media will be as significant as it is today in ten years. What I can say is its significance in our market is unmatched. This means that Millennials, or even those that come after them, will drive for more use and understanding of this technology. All others will be left to learn proper and effective integration without upsetting their businesses foundation. Online success does not mean a dismissal of the business practices that worked well for decades, such as phone communication and interpersonal connectivity; but it means finding a proper way to embrace the technology and meet the demand of the next generation.

As was previously stated, the best way to see a return on your invested time in online communication is to add value to your individual marketplace through effective content creation and delivery. Remember, your website is the foundational element to showcase your business, but social media is the way to prove that you deliver on your promises. Too many people think that if something appears too insignificant to them that it will not add value to a digital world. But I promise you that the digital world is filled with much more insignificance than what you would ever publish. Something that may seem insignificant to you may be tremendously valuable to someone else. In social media and online communication, you are not pandering to one audience, you are pandering to many. What holds less value to one audience is the most valuable to another. It is impossible to determine what the online community will find valuable and effective on a day to day basis, especially in the Millennial market. So, it is in your best interest to not limit content and ensure that a stream of connectivity is present.

Something that many businesses sometimes forget is that although people will go to social media to learn about the real, tangible value of a company, at some point, they are going to want to connect with you. Ensure that your social media accounts all have the same contact information on them. This may be the link to your website, a phone number, or a link to other social accounts. Think about what is going to provide the most seamless transition from research to action for a potential client or customer.

How important is being right?

Ask yourself this question: "How important is it to me that I am right?" Sometimes it is easy for us to be right in our approach, meaning that someone else is, naturally, wrong. This happens a lot between generations. One generation wants to think their way of doing something is "right" and are not willing to take a step back for any other consideration. This goes both ways. Millennials feel that their ways of doing things and their approach is best, and it may be best for them. But sometimes it is not about being right, but rather about what works best. For example, if a Millennial will not return your calls and only communicates through email and text, it does not mean they are correct, but in the moment, your mentality is skewed by right vs. wrong. In this example, their way worked for both parties although it may not have been the chosen method of both parties. Sometimes we get our way; sometimes we don't. The notion of "can't" often comes to play when looking at generations in terms of right and wrong. A Baby Boomer may determine they can't work with Millennials because they assume Millennials are always wrong. But, sometimes being right is not always the most important consideration. Equally, Millennials may find that they can't achieve in the same ways as someone of an older generation. If their perception of right vs. wrong is altered, they realize that achievement is attainable, but it comes with a different measure of success.

It is necessary to continually remember that we all want to be right. But sometimes, our right is someone else's wrong. Keep in mind, respect goes both ways.

Tell Your (And Your Company's) Story

We all have a story to tell about why we do what we do and how we became involved. What amazes most people is that Millennials love these stories. These stories help distinguish you from your competition. It goes back to being able to showcase yourself in a way that adds value to you and your business. The way you approach your story is no different. Millennials want relationships with people and to do business with companies that have a story. Millennials will do business with a company once for the ease of access, but they will not stay loyal to them. They will do business with a company multiple times and develop loyalty if that company shows that they believe in something more than ease of access. The businesses that succeed most among this group are the ones with faces. We can all name organizations that have no face and no story. Don't be that business. Your story is interesting because it is unique to you and your company. No two stories are the same.

Outsmart The Consumer

Let's face it, the Millennial generation is smart and full of questions. Remember, this is the group that has been encouraged their entire lives to ask questions regardless of relevance. They are also the most educated group of people ever. Knowing this, it is important to remember that they will ask questions; lots of questions. They want to know about the companies they are doing business with and the products or services they are consuming. They will try to trip you up, so don't let them. In order to be properly prepared, you need to have answers to questions you have never been asked. Millennials are cost-conscious, respectful of their environment, and curious about the mark they are leaving on the world. They will keep these things in mind when doing business. It is in the best interest of business owners and managers to prepare for the toughest of questions.

The best way to prepare for a challenging consumer market is to outsmart them. You are the knowledge expert in your respective field. You must take it upon yourself to out-think everyone you are doing business with. You may have the best product, service or idea, but against an inquisitive audience, nothing but proper answers to their inquiries will help. To do this, you must first understand that you are the expert and you hold the keys. Then, you must expand on your personal knowledge as an expert representative in your field. If a Millennial asks how your business impacts the environment, give them an honest answer, even if that answer is not what you think they want to hear. Any answer is better than no answer.

It is also vital to keep up your respective industry knowledge. We all have opportunities to expand our industry knowledge on a continuous basis. It has become even more critical to take advantage of these opportunities to learn and expand. Thanks to the present level of online connectivity, information about anything and everything is available to consumers. Most consumers have a basic search engine knowledge of the consumerism world. There is a constant need to ensure that nothing unnecessarily challenges a business. To do that, one must stay mindful of any updates or changes to a marketplace that may affect their industry.

Don't Assume To Know Millennials

It has been said again and again in this book, but the most import strategy when dealing with Millennials (or anyone really) is to remove assumption. Don't assume to know Millennials and they won't assume to know you. This is not always a negative assumption either. Some people find that they have relatability with Millennials and that they really know them. But, it's important to remember that unless you are a Millennial, you can not really understand Millennials, just like I can never really understand a Baby Boomer because there is no way I can be a Baby Boomer.

Perceptions and assumptions are among the most harmful interferences in the generational breakdown. It is very easy to create assumptions about someone else based on your involvement with one of their peers. Yes, we all know "those Millennials"; the ones who evoke entitlement and narcissism. However, that is not the embodiment of the Millennial generation as a whole. Assuming that one Millennial speaks for all is like assuming that one Baby Boomer represents the entire generation. The truth is we are all different and unique. You will inevitably interact with "those Millennials", but I guarantee you will come across "those Baby Boomers" and "those Gen X'ers", too. We all have our shortcomings, and some of our peers make them more recognizable. It is easy to place a label on a Millennial based on presumptions, but that can just as easily be reversed.

Finally, and absolutely the most important thing, no matter who you are or what demographic you identify with, is to remember that respect goes both ways. No matter what age group I speak to, I always close with this thought. It is easy to forget to be respectful of one another. Millennials, like anyone else, respond to respect and will also easily reciprocate that respect.

Want Seth to present to your company or at your conference?

Visit
www.TheSeasonedGroup.com

CPSIA information can be obtained
at www.ICGtesting.com
Printed in the USA
FFOW03n1014241117
43703341-42592FF